BEETLES

Adele D. Richardson

It's daytime. In a **HOT**, dry desert a small insect sits atop a sand dune. The sun **BEATS** down upon its shiny body. After a moment the insect *burrows* under the sand to cool itself off. In a different part of the world, at the same time, another

BEETLES

Published by Smart Apple Media

123 South Broad Street

Mankato, Minnesota 56001

Photos: Guy Bruyea (cover, pages 2–3, 6–9, 11, 21, 22–24);

Frank Peairs (pages 13, 14, 16); John Capinera (pages 18,

19, 25); Whitney Cranshaw (pages 20, 26, 28); Dave

Leatherman (page 17, 27); Entomological Society of

America/Ries Memorial Slide Collection (pages 10,

12, 15)

Design &Production: EvansDay Design

Project management: Odyssey Books

Library of Congress Cataloging-in-Publication Data

Richardson, Adele, 1966–

Beetles / Adele Richardson. – 1st ed.

Includes bibliographical references and index.

Summary: Describes the habitat, life cycle, behavior,

predators, and unique characteristics of beetles.

ISBN 1-887068-30-9 (alk. paper)

1. Beetles—Juvenile literature. [1. Beetles.] I. Title.

II. Series: Bugs (Mankato, Minn.)

QL576.2.R535 1998

595.76—dc21   98-15345

First Edition   9 8 7 6 5 4 3 2 1

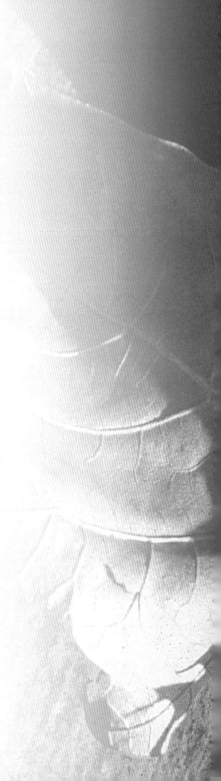

INSECT *whirls crazily* IN A SHALLOW POND. IN YET ANOTHER LAND, A THIRD INSECT **POKES** ITS HEAD OUT FROM THE BARK OF A TREE AND TAKES A LOOK AROUND. THESE INSECTS ALL HAVE ONE THING IN COMMON. THEY'RE **BEETLES!** AND THEY ARE *everywhere!*

A Beetle World

There are more SPECIES, or kinds, of beetles than of any other animal group in the world. So far scientists have named well over 300,000 different beetles, and there are perhaps thousands more out there that haven't been discovered yet. In fact, if you lined up all of the animals in the world, every fourth one would be a beetle.

Beetles are very important to our world. Many species remove unwanted dead animals and plants, damaging insects, and even DUNG (animal droppings) from the environment. This may be

A beetle is right at home on a plant leaf.

one reason why there are so many beetles—they eat just about anything!

Beetles can live just about anywhere, except in the oceans and Antarctica. They live in obvious places, such as in woodlands, under rocks, on plants, and in caves. But others have been found where you wouldn't think an insect could survive—deserts, streams and ponds, and even the cold Arctic. They also like to live where humans live. Sometimes they are even in our carpets.

Many Sizes and Colors

Beetles come in many sizes. One of the largest is the Hercules beetle (*Dynastes hercules*), which lives in Central America. It can grow to be 7 inches (17.5 cm) long! The smallest beetles are no bigger than a dot made by a sharp pencil.

Beetles also come in many colors. Most people think of them as being black or brown. But there are beetles colored in shiny green, yellow, blue, and even gold.

In some countries, like Australia, people use beetles with metallic-looking bodies (green is a favorite color) to make jewelry and hair ornaments.

Bodies of Beetles

The scientific name for beetles is *Coleoptera*. It comes from two Greek words: *koleos*, which means "sheath," and *ptera*, which means "wings." This describes the hard, shiny armor that protects their bodies.

Like all insects, beetles have six legs and breathe air. Their bodies are divided into three sections: head, thorax, and abdomen.

A beetle's armor makes it the toughest bug in the insect world.

The head of every beetle is perfectly suited for its lifestyle.

Head The head of a beetle has eyes, antennae, and mouthparts. The eyes can be large or small, depending on where the insect lives. A good example of this is the whirligig (family *Gyrinidae*), a beetle that lives in fresh water. Each of its eyes is large and split in two, so it actually has four eyes. Half of each eye is located on the bottom of its head. This is so the beetle can see straight down into the water and keep a lookout for food or enemies.

Beetles that hunt often have large eyes to see their prey. Cave-dwelling beetles that live in darkness may be completely blind or may have very small eyes.

The ANTENNAE, or feelers, are even more important than the eyes. Beetles use them to smell as well as touch. The longhorn beetle *(Cyrambycidae)* received its name because of the size of its antennae. The Hercules beetle is one of this species. Its "horn" (or antennae) can be over

3 inches (7.5 cm) long! Scientists believe that some of these beetles use their long antennae to help them keep their balance while walking across twigs and branches.

The males of a species of beetle called the *phengodes*, or "railroad worms," have antennae that are very large and feathery.

Beetle Jaws The shape of a beetle's mouthparts greatly depends on the foods it eats. For example, beetles that eat plants and leaves have MANDIBLES, or jaws, that look similar to a pair of scissors. Hunter beetles—the type that eats animals and other insects—have long, sharp jaws that resemble pincers.

Look closely at the jaws of this scarab beetle. Does it eat plants or other insects?

The males of a species called stag beetles (*Lucanidae*) have huge jaws that look like deer antlers. They are used mostly for fighting. The females also have these "antlers," but theirs are not quite so large.

Weevil beetles (family *Curculionidae*) have long "snouts" with jaws at the end for their mouths. These "snouts" are often used for biting into hard materials like seeds and nutshells.

The horns of this chafer beetle (family Scarabaeidae) are nearly as long as its head.

Thorax   The beetle's four wings and six legs are located at the THORAX, or middle section. The outer wings, called ELYTRA, are what set the beetle apart from other insects. They act as a hard and often colorful covering that protects the rear wings (if there are any—not all beetles fly) and the abdomen. Beetles do not flap their elytra much. Most of the time they are held straight out, like the wings of an airplane. This helps give the beetles direction while their rear wings do most of the work.

The rear wings are very long and delicate. When not in use, the beetle keeps them folded up and protected underneath its elytra. Most beetles will climb to the tip

Beetle Legs

The type of legs a beetle has depends on its lifestyle. Beetles that burrow (family *Silphidae*) have short, thick legs for digging. The legs of ground beetles *(Carabide)* are long and slender so the insect can move quickly while hunting. They also have a special feature called antennae-cleaners. These are tiny sections in the middle of the front legs that are lined with bristles. The beetle will run its antennae through this section to remove any dirt that has built up. Imagine a beetle grooming itself!

of a leaf or a blade of grass before they take off. They do this so their wings don't hit the ground and become damaged.

In the few species that don't fly, the elytra are fused together. This makes their armor even stronger and gives them the appearance of little tanks.

Abdomen The ABDOMEN is the third section of a beetle's body. Here is where its digestive system, reproductive organs, and respiratory system are located. When a beetle eats, the food moves from its mouth to a muscular tube called a GIZZARD. The gizzard crushes the food into smaller pieces so the beetle can finish digesting it. Inside the gizzard are stiff hairs that allow only the smaller pieces to pass through. If a piece is too big, it will stay for further grinding.

After food has passed through the gizzard, the beetle's body removes the nutrients and water it needs to stay alive. Whatever is left moves into the intestines and is eliminated from the body as waste.

A Perfect Fit Beetle abdomens vary from species to species. The reproductive organs of one type of beetle will not fit into the body of another species. This is

The elytra of most beetles are colorful as well as protective.

nature's way of making sure only beetles of the same species mate together.

Beetles breathe through little airholes in their abdomens. If they live in water, beetles can store air under their elytra and absorb it through these airholes as they need it. This makes beetles nature's scuba divers!

It's a Beetle's Life

A beetle goes through four different stages of development in its lifetime. The stages are egg, larva, pupa, and adult. This process is called METAMORPHOSIS, which means "change of form." Though the first stage is the egg, the life cycle really begins with the adult and its search for a mate.

Mating   Since there are so many different species of beetles, they don't all use the same method to attract mates. Some

This soldier beetle offers a peek at its usually hidden abdomen.

Mating is an important part of a beetle's life cycle.

produce chemicals, called PHEROMONES. Others, like the firefly (family *Lampyridae*), light up or glow. You may be most familiar with the common firefly *(Photinus tany-toxus)*, which is not really a fly, but a beetle. The deathwatch beetle (family *Ptinidae*) calls out to a female by tapping its head on a piece of wood.

Once a female is found, the male places an organ called an AEDEAGUS inside of her and fertilizes her eggs.

Egg Stage   After mating is complete, the female will find a food supply for her young and lay the eggs. Beetle eggs can be large or small, depending on the species of beetle. You can determine the type of beetle the eggs will become by where they are

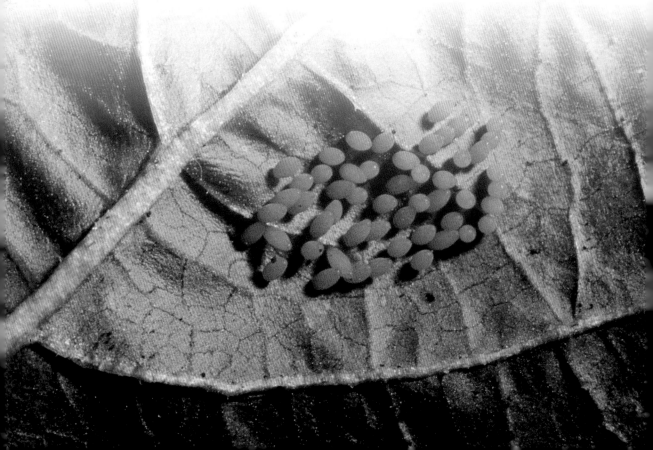

found. Dung beetles *(Scarabaes sacer)* roll cow droppings into little balls. The eggs are placed inside the dung ball and buried in the ground. The dung is what the babies eat after they hatch!

Larva Stage   A baby beetle becomes a LARVA at the second stage of metamorphosis. Larvae are worm-like in appearance and are also known as grubs. Beetle larvae do all their growing during this time of their lives. That's why they're so hungry.

The bodies of larvae do not expand as they grow,

The underside of a leaf is a safe hiding place for beetle eggs.

Egg Hiding Places

Leaf beetles *(Chrysomelidae)* often roll a leaf around their eggs for food and protection. The oak weevil *(Cucujiformia)*, which is a species of beetle, drills a hole in an acorn and lays her eggs there. When they hatch, the hungry babies will eat away at the inside of the nut.

and their skins become too small to hold their bodies. When this happens they MOLT, or shed their skin. The old skin splits and the larva simply wriggles out wearing a new skin on a slightly larger body. Larvae will go through 3 to 14 molts, depending on the species and how much food is available. After the final molt, the larvae are ready for the pupa stage.

Pupa Stage Many species of beetle larvae will burrow into the ground before becoming a PUPA. Others, such as members of wood-boring families *(Buprestoidea)*,

hide inside of wood. Water beetle larvae (family *Dytiscidae*) come to land and dig a hole in the ground to hide.

In this stage a beetle stops eating and becomes very inactive. It grows a tough outer skin over its body and waits for its adult body to develop. When it's finally ready, the beetle chews its way through the covering and crawls out. It is usually very light in color, and after a few hours in the air its body will harden and darken in color. Then it has officially made it to adulthood.

🐞 | *These hungry larvae eat so much food they grow right out of their skins.*

Beetle Self-Defense

Beetles are considered food by birds, frogs, snakes, and other animals. Their body armor is a good defense against these hungry PREDATORS, but many beetles use other tactics to avoid becoming someone's dinner.

Click beetles (*Elateridae*) are masters of surprise. When approached by an enemy, the first thing they do is "play dead." If this doesn't work, they use a spring-like feature between the thorax and abdomen and jump into the air—as

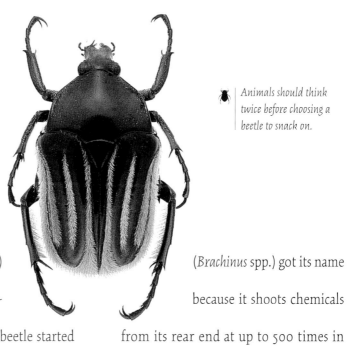

much as 14 inches (35 cm) high! Imagine how surprised a frog would be if a beetle started jumping around inside its mouth! Flea beetles *(Chrysomelidae)* can jump up to 2 feet (61 cm) for a quick getaway.

Chemical Warfare Blister beetles *(Meloidae)* are one species that uses bright colors to warn predators away. If a predator is still foolish enough to come close, the insect releases a chemical that burns the skin. The bombardier beetle *(Brachinus* spp.) got its name because it shoots chemicals from its rear end at up to 500 times in one second!

One species that has a startling defense is the bloody nose beetle *(Timarcha tenebricosa)*. When threatened, it spills out a red liquid that makes it look like it has a bloody nose. The pretty ladybug *(Coccinelidae)*, which is actually a beetle, squirts out a smelly, yellow liquid from its leg joints. This liquid can be poisonous to some animals.

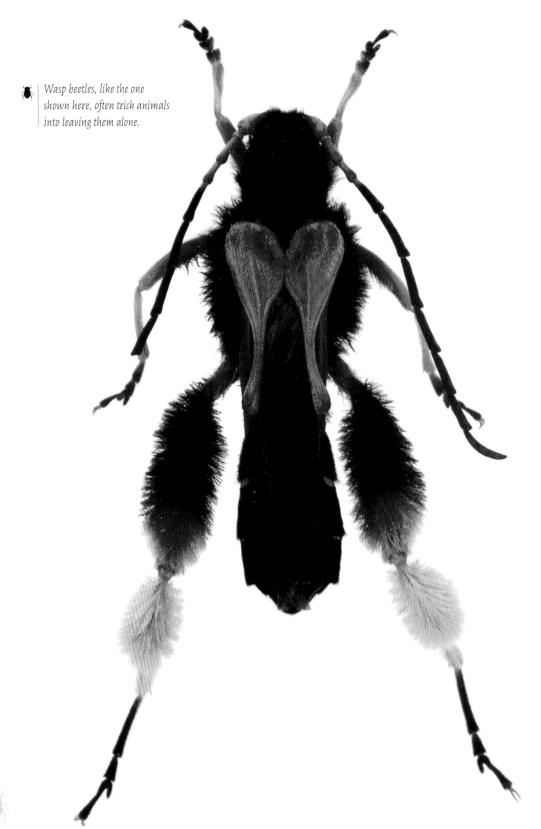

Wasp beetles, like the one shown here, often trick animals into leaving them alone.

Copycats   Some beetles can imitate other insects. The wasp beetle (family *Cerambycidae*) earned its name because it has the same colorings that a wasp does. Because of this, many predators will simply leave it alone for fear of being stung.

Another imitator is the devil's coach horse (family *Cerambycidae*), also known as the cocktail beetle. This insect raises up its rear end so it looks like a stinging insect, such as a scorpion. If this tactic doesn't work, the beetle emits an awful smell to chase away its enemy.

Most beetles rely on a defense tactic as well as their tough elytra to keep them safe.

Masters of Disguise

Beetles CAMOUFLAGE themselves to blend in with their surroundings. In Africa there is a rare darkling beetle (family *Tenebrionidae*) with completely white elytra. These enable the insect to partially burrow into sand and not be seen.

The brown-colored seed beetle (family *Bruchidae*) gets its name because during the day, it allows itself to be blown around by the wind, just like a real seed. Many times a predator will not even realize that its dinner just blew by!

With all this self-defense it's no wonder beetles have survived so well!

Beetles as Pests

Many beetles are considered very important in nature because of what they eat. Sexton beetles (*Nicrophorus vespillo*) are SCAVENGERS, or trash collectors. They can remove the earth from underneath a dead animal until it is buried. Then, both the young and adult beetles eat it. Dung beetles are just as useful in removing cow droppings.

Not all beetles are so considerate. Many are thought of as pests and can cause a lot of damage. For example, Colorado potato

The Colorado potato beetle is a little bug with a big appetite.

beetles (*Leptinotarsa decemlineata*) eat potato plants, and lots of them. If left alone, they can eat a whole crop of potatoes in just one year.

Another serious pest is the cotton boll weevil (family *Curculionidae*). Some experts believe that these insects eat more than $20 million worth of cotton in one year!

Beetles in the House   Some of the pest beetles you may find in the house are flour and carpet beetles (both family *Dermestidae*). Their names can tell you what they like to eat. The adult carpet beetles don't actually eat the carpet, though. Their hungry larvae do all the damage.

Another household pest is the wood-

Hungry beetles can totally destroy a plant.

worm beetle (family *Scolytidae*). The larvae of this insect burrow into and eat deadwood. Since most furniture is made from wood, you can imagine what a pest this bug can be. The woodworm will go through its pupa stage inside the wood and exit as an adult through a tiny hole. If you discover the hole with sawdust around it, it's too late! The damage has already been done.

Fortunately, not all homes are infested with beetles. These are just a few of the types that may try to get in. Now that you know what they eat, you can keep a lookout for them.

Engraver beetles spend their lives tunneling under tree bark.

Discover Beetles for Yourself

After learning about all the different beetles in the world, you may want to discover for yourself which beetles are in your neighborhood—and maybe even keep a few so you can watch their life cycle. But how do you catch them?

The best time to beetle hunt is on a sunny day. Try looking under rocks or on plants. You may even want to build a trap to catch a few specimens. This is easy to do. Start by burying a plastic cup until the rim is level with the ground. Set a couple

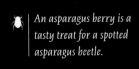
An asparagus berry is a tasty treat for a spotted asparagus beetle.

of rocks around it and cover it with a piece of wood. Put some food in the cup as bait, and there is a good chance that you will catch a beetle. If you do make a trap, make sure to take it apart when you're finished, so that another curious beetle doesn't come along and get stuck inside.

A Beetle Home   Beetles make interesting pets. If you decide to keep them, you will need a cage, such as a TERRARIUM, or dry aquarium, with dirt, wood, and rocks in the bottom. Make sure it has a tight lid with a mesh covering. The dirt in the bottom must be moist or your beetles could dry out. And they must have food.

Once your beetles are in the terrarium, place it on a shaded windowsill. Above all, make sure your beetles are the same species or they might eat each other!

Raising Ladybugs

Ladybugs are a popular beetle to raise. First, find a plant with the larvae on it. Ladybug larvae look like little copies of the adults, except they have no wings or elytra yet. If you are able to find the larvae, put the whole plant in the terrarium. It won't take long, and you'll be able to watch metamorphosis!

One final note on collecting beetles: When you release your beetles back into nature, always make sure you put them back where you found them. Beetles usually stay close to a food source. If you put them back somewhere different, they may starve to death.

Becoming a Beetle Expert Collecting or even just watching beetles can be a fun and interesting hobby. You may even become a beetle expert!

Though you may not notice them, beetles are all around us. Next time you go outside, take a closer look and see how many beetles you can find. There are thousands of species out there for you to discover!

BOOKS

Amazing Beetles, John Still, Alfred A. Knopf, 1991

Beetles, Sylvia Johnson, Lerner Publications, 1982

Beetles and How They Live, Dorothy Hinshaw Patent and Paul C. Schroeder, Holiday House, 1978

Discovering Beetles, Malcolm Penny, The Bookwright Press, 1986

I Like Beetles, Gladys Conklin, Holiday House, 1975

Insects in Armor: A Beetle Book, Ross E. Hutchins, Parents Magazine Press, 1972

Keeping Minibeasts: Beetles, Barrie Watts, Franklin Watts Publishers, 1989

CHAPTERS IN BOOKS

The Big Bug Book, Margery Facklam, Little, Brown and Company, 1994, p. 28

Busy Bugs: Burying Beetle, Ada and Frank Graham, Dodd, Mead and Company, 1983

Insects, Elizabeth Cooper, Steck-Vaughn Company, 1990

Insects, Alice Fields, Franklin Watts, 1980, pp. 8–9, 43

Weird and Wonderful Insects, Sue Hadden, Thompson Learning, 1993

FIELD GUIDES

The Amateur Naturalist, Gerald Durrell (naturalist), H. Hamilton Publishers, 1986

Discovering the Outdoors, a Nature and Science Guide, American Museum of Natural History, 1969

Eyewitness–Living Earth, Miranda Smith, DK Publishers, 1996

The Living Community, a Venture into Ecology, S. Carl Hirsch, Viking Press, 1966, pp. 12, 38, 71

Simon & Schuster Guide to Insects, Ross H. Arnett, Jr. and Richard L. Jacques, Jr., Simon and Schuster, 1981

WEB

"Beetles," Entomology Department, Iowa State University, 1998

"Beetles Research," University of London, 1997

"Bug Club Home Page," Amateur Entomologists Society, 1997

"Coleoptera," Insect Compendium Index, 1997

"Image Gallery at BioHaven," Guy Bruyea (entomologist), 1998

"Insects Home Page," Gordon Ramel (entomologist), 1997

ENCYCLOPEDIAS

Compton's Encyclopedia online

Encyclopedia of Wildlife, Castle Books, 1974

Grzimek's Animal Life Encyclopedia, Vol. 2, *Insects*, Van Nostrand Reinhold Co., 1974

Nature Encyclopedia, Martyn Bramwell, Warwick Press, 1989

Nature Encyclopedia, Checkerboard Press, 1989

The New Book of Knowledge, Vol. 2, Grolier, 1997

NSA Family Encyclopedia, Vol. 3, Standard Educational Company, 1993

The World Book Encyclopedia, Vol. 2, World Book, 1997

MAGAZINE ARTICLES

"Beetle Mania: An Attraction to Fire," *Bioscience*, January 1998, p. 3

"Boom Time for Beetles," *New Scientist*, November 1997, p. 19

"Clean Up Your Act, or the Bugs May Take Over," *Pest Control*, November 1997, p. 78

"Snout Beetles to the Rescue," *Wildlife Conservation*, December 1997, p. 14

"That Crunchy Stuff in Your Cereal Bowl May Not Be Granola," *Wall Street Journal*, Eastern Edition, November 3, 1997, p. A1

"Warning: This Bug May Scare You Silly," *Arizona Highways*, November 1997, p. 36

MUSEUMS

California Academy of Sciences
Golden Gate Park
San Francisco, CA

The Milwaukee Public Museum
Milwaukee, WI

Natural History Museum
of Los Angeles County
Los Angeles, CA

Smithsonian Institution
Washington, DC

I N D E X

A
abdomen 8, 12, 13, 20–21
aedeagus 16
antennae (feelers) 9–10, 12

C
camouflage 24
Coleoptera 8

D
defense mechanisms 9, 20–23
diet 7, 13, 17, 25–26

E
eggs 15, 16–17
enemies 9, 20
eyes 9

F
families
  Bruchidae 24
  Buprestoidae 18
  Carabidae 12
  Cerambycidae 23
  Chrysomelidae 17, 21
  Coccinelidae 21
  Cucujiformia 17
  Curculionidae 11, 26
  Cyrambycidae 9
  Dermestidae 26
  Dytiscidae 19
  Elateridae 20
  Gyrinidae 9
  Lampyridae 16
  Lucanidae 11
  Meloidae 21
  Ptinidae 16
  Scarabaeidae 11
  Scolytidae 27

  Silphidae 12
  Tenebrionidae 24

G
gizzard 13

H
habitat 7
hunting 9

L
larvae 15, 17–18, 26
legs 8, 12

M
mating 14, 15–16
metamorphosis 15, 17, 30
molt 18
mouth/jaws 9, 10–11
  mandibles 10

P
pheromones 16
predators 20, 21, 23
pupa 15, 18–19, 27

S
scavengers 25
species
  asparagus beetle 28
  blister beetle 21
  bloody nose beetle (*Timarcha tenebricosa*) 21
  bombardier beetle (*Brachinus spp.*) 21
  carpet beetle 26
  chafer beetle 11
  click beetle 20–21
  cocktail beetle OR devil's coach horse 23

  Colorado potato beetle (*Leptinotarsa decemlineata*) 25–26
  common firefly (*Photinus tanytoxus*) 16
  cotton boll weevil 26
  darkling beetle 24
  deathwatch beetle 16
  devil's coach horse OR cocktail beetle 23
  dung beetle (*Scarabaes sacer*) 17
  engraver beetle 27
  firefly 16
  flea beetle 21
  flour beetle 26
  Hercules beetle (*Dynastes hercules*) 9–10
  ladybug 21, 30
  leaf beetle 17
  long-horn beetle 9–10
  Mexican bean beetle 19
  oak weevil 17
  phengodes (railroad worm) 10
  scarab beetle 10
  seed beetle 24
  sexton beetle (*Nicrophorus vespillo*) 25
  soldier beetle 15
  stag beetle 11
  wasp beetle 22, 23
  water beetle 19
  weevil beetle 11
  whirligig 9
  wood-boring beetle 18–19
  woodworm beetle 26–27

T
terrarium 29, 30
thorax 12, 20

W
wings 12–13, 30
  elytra 12–13, 14, 24, 30